# The Illustrated Rosary
—FOR CHILDREN—

Written
Sr. Karen Cavanaugh

Illustrated by
William Luberoff

Regina
Press

# Why We Pray the Rosary

The Rosary is a special way of praying to God that honors Mary, the Mother of Jesus. As we recite the prayers of the Rosary, we think about certain stories in the lives of Jesus and Mary.

These stories are called "mysteries":— a mystery is a story about God and God's life in another person. We use Rosary beads to help us keep count of the prayers and the mysteries.

The complete Rosary consists of fifteen decades. There are three sets of mysteries and five stories in each set.

When we use the Rosary beads, we pray five decades and one set of mysteries at a time.

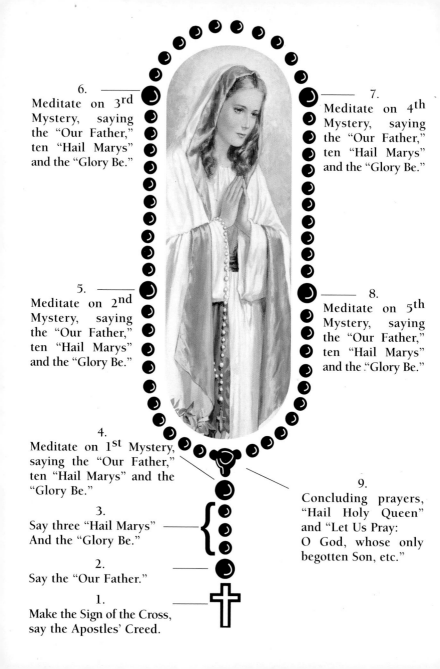

**6.** ——
Meditate on 3$^{rd}$ Mystery, saying the "Our Father," ten "Hail Marys" and the "Glory Be."

—— **7.**
Meditate on 4$^{th}$ Mystery, saying the "Our Father," ten "Hail Marys" and the "Glory Be."

**5.** ——
Meditate on 2$^{nd}$ Mystery, saying the "Our Father," ten "Hail Marys" and the "Glory Be."

—— **8.**
Meditate on 5$^{th}$ Mystery, saying the "Our Father," ten "Hail Marys" and the "Glory Be."

**4.**
Meditate on 1$^{st}$ Mystery, saying the "Our Father," ten "Hail Marys" and the "Glory Be."

**9.**
Concluding prayers, "Hail Holy Queen" and "Let Us Pray: O God, whose only begotten Son, etc."

**3.**
Say three "Hail Marys" And the "Glory Be."

**2.**
Say the "Our Father."

**1.**
Make the Sign of the Cross, say the Apostles' Creed.

# How We Pray the Rosary

Rosary beads are used to keep count of the prayers and mysteries. Recite the Apostles' Creed while you hold the crucifix, then one Our Father and three Hail Marys. After that, as you think about each mystery, recite the Our Father on the large bead, the Hail Mary on each of ten smaller beads and finish with a Glory Be. That makes one decade. The complete Rosary consists of five decades. There are three sets of mysteries and five stories in each set.

## THE GLORY BE

Glory be to the Father
and to the Son
and to the Holy Spirit,
as it was in the beginning,
is now and ever shall be,
world without end. Amen.

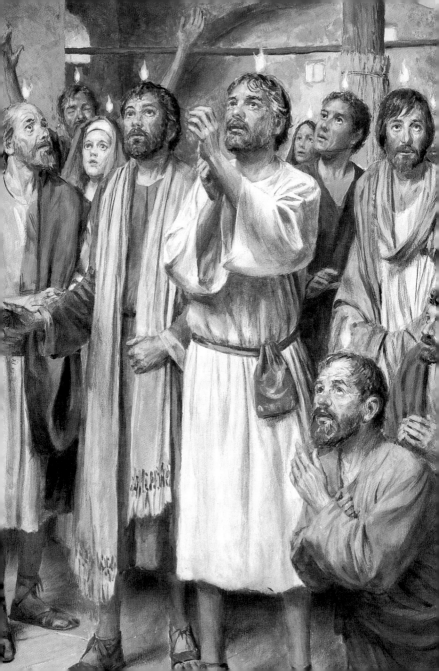

# The Apostles' Creed

I believe in God, the Father almighty,
creator of heaven and earth.
I believe in Jesus Christ, his only Son,
our Lord. He was conceived
by the power of the Holy Spirit
and born of the Virgin Mary.
He suffered under Pontius Pilate,
was crucified, died, and was buried.
He descended to the dead.
On the third day he rose again.
He ascended into heaven,
and is seated at the right hand
of the Father.
He will come again
to judge the living and the dead.
I believe in the Holy Spirit,
the holy Catholic Church,
the communion of saints,
the forgiveness of sins,
the resurrection of the body,
and the life everlasting. Amen.

## THE OUR FATHER

Our Father, who art in heaven,
hallowed be thy name.
Thy kingdom come.
Thy will be done on earth,
as it is in heaven.
Give us this day our daily bread,
and forgive us our trespasses,
as we forgive those
who trespass against us,
and lead us not into temptation,
but deliver us from evil. Amen.

## THE HAIL MARY

Hail Mary, full of grace,
the Lord is with you;
blessed are you among women,
and blessed is the fruit
of your womb, Jesus.
Holy Mary, Mother of God,
pray for us sinners now
and at the hour of our death. Amen.

# The Mysteries of the Rosary

There are three sets of mysteries, or stories, for us to think about while we pray the Rosary. The stories tell of Mary's time with Jesus, her Son.

The stories are the five Joyful Mysteries (see page 13), the five Sorrowful Mysteries (see page 19) and the five Glorious Mysteries (see page 25).

We usually pray the Joyful Mysteries on Mondays and Thursdays. On Tuesdays and Fridays, we pray the Sorrowful Mysteries. The Glorious Mysteries are usually prayed on Wednesdays, Saturdays, and Sundays.

Sometimes people pray just one decade of the Rosary at a time. Some people pray all fifteen decades in a single day.

# The Joyful Mysteries

The Joyful Mysteries of the Rosary remind us of the joyful, happy times in the lives of Jesus and Mary. When we pray the Rosary, we imagine five of those times.

The Joyful stories, or mysteries, which we remember are:

1. **THE ANNUNCIATION**
The coming of Jesus is announced

2. **THE VISITATION**
Mary visits her cousin, Elizabeth

3. **THE NATIVITY**
Jesus is born

4. **THE PRESENTATION**
Jesus is Presented to God

5. **THE FINDING IN THE TEMPLE**
Jesus is found after being lost

# 1. THE ANNUNCIATION

We imagine and remember how Mary was asked to be the Mother of God. She said "Yes" to God's special invitation, and the child Jesus began to live and grow inside her body.

Although she was a little bit frightened, Mary trusted God's request. She prayed that she would be a good mother.

# 2. THE VISITATION

Now we picture Mary going to visit Elizabeth, her cousin. They would each become the mother of a special person.

Mary's Son would be Jesus, our Savior.

Elizabeth's son would be John, who would later become "the Baptist." John the Baptist would preach the coming of the Savior.

## 3. THE NATIVITY

It is easy to imagine the scene of Jesus' birth in a stable at Bethlehem. Mary and her husband, Joseph, lovingly welcome Jesus into their lives. They dream of the wonderful things they will show him, and they promise to care for him.

## 4. THE PRESENTATION

We picture Mary and Joseph bringing their infant son to the Temple. Here they thank God for their baby and promise to love and cherish him. As good Jewish parents, they offer their child to God. They also promise to teach him about God, who cares for us all.

## 5. THE FINDING IN THE TEMPLE

We recall another Temple scene when Jesus was a young boy. Jesus had stayed behind after the Temple service to talk to the priests and teachers. Mary and Joseph thought he was lost. When they found him, they were filled with joy and thanked God.

# The Sorrowful Mysteries

The Gospels also tell us that when Jesus was still a baby his mother was told that he would be rejected and her heart would be broken. In the Sorrowful Mysteries of the Rosary, we remember five of the most sorrowful times in the lives of Mary and Jesus.

The Sorrowful Mysteries are:

1. **JESUS' AGONY IN THE GARDEN**
Jesus prays in the Garden of Olives

2. **THE SCOURGING AT THE PILLAR**
Jesus is beaten and whipped

3. **THE CROWNING WITH THORNS**
Jesus has a crown of thorns put on his head

4. **JESUS CARRIES HIS CROSS**
Jesus carries his cross to Calvary

5. **THE CRUCIFIXION**
Jesus dies on the cross

# 1. Jesus' Agony in the Garden

Jesus knew that he had been betrayed by his own friend and rejected by the Jewish leaders. We can remember and imagine him talking to God. We picture him after his Last Supper going to pray in a garden. Knowing that his enemies are near, he is frightened, cold, and sweaty. He does not want to die but finds the strength and courage to die for us.

# 2. The Scourging at the Pillar

The Roman procurator, Pilate, orders Jesus to be whipped and beaten. We can picture the soldiers carrying out this command.

Jesus was badly beaten by the soldiers. He silently accepted this sorrow and pain out of love for all humankind.

## 3. THE CROWNING WITH THORNS

We try to imagine now the hurt, bleeding Jesus being mocked. Jesus' hands are tied. A purple cloth is put on his shoulders and a crown of thorns put upon his head. The soldiers dance around him, spit at him, and call him king.

## 4. JESUS CARRIES HIS CROSS

We picture Jesus carrying a rough, heavy wooden cross to Calvary, where he will die. Along the way, he meets his heartbroken mother and friends. They cry as sorrow fills them.

## 5. THE CRUCIFIXION

Imagine Jesus' mother now. Her child is hanging, nailed to a cross, and slowly dying. While he is dying, He asks God to forgive everyone, and then he gives his spirit over to God.

With all his being, Jesus showed his love for us.

# The Glorious Mysteries

Jesus and Mary were given special glories because they were faithful to God. When we pray the Glorious Mysteries, we imagine five of those times.

The Glorious Mysteries of the Rosary are:

1. **THE RESURRECTION**
   Jesus rises from the dead

2. **THE ASCENSION**
   Jesus returns to heaven

3. **THE DESCENT OF THE HOLY SPIRIT**
   Jesus sends his spirit

4. **THE ASSUMPTION OF MARY**
   Mary is taken to heaven

5. **THE CROWNING OF MARY**
   Mary is crowned Queen of Heaven

## 1. THE RESURRECTION

We picture Jesus coming forth from the tomb on Easter Sunday morning. Jesus' rising from the dead brings with it a promise of new life for us. Jesus has conquered death for ever.

## 2. THE ASCENSION

Imagine the friends and followers of Jesus as they watched him being lifted out of their sight. Jesus had taught them everything they needed to know, and he now returns to God's presence — heaven.

## 3. THE DESCENT OF THE HOLY SPIRIT

We remember that Jesus promised that he would never leave his friends alone. We call to mind that on Pentecost Jesus' followers were filled with the power of the Holy Spirit. Their hearts received God's peace and energy.

## 4. The Assumption of Mary

Just as Mary loved her son, so did Jesus have a very special love for his mother. Because of this special love, she was taken to heaven body and spirit when she died. We can picture her in heaven with Jesus as she tells us how glorious heaven is. From heaven, Mary cares for us, as her children.

## 5. The Crowning of Mary

Not only does Jesus want his mother to be in heaven with Him but he prepares a special place for her.

We imagine the angels and the holy souls around the throne of God, all of them glorifying God, as Jesus welcomes Mary to the center of heaven.

He crowns her Queen of Heaven. She is now our Queen and the Queen of the Universe.

# Mary and the Rosary

We are taught that throughout history Mary has appeared and encouraged us to pray the Rosary.

In the beginning of the thirteenth century Mary appeared to Saint Dominic and gave him a Rosary. Dominic taught the people how to say the Rosary and to pray for God's blessings.

At Lourdes in France, Mary appeared to Saint Bernadette eighteen times between February and July, 1858. Mary called for penance and said, "I am the Immaculate Conception." Many miracles still take place at Lourdes, where each day thousands of people pray the Rosary.

In 1917, Mary appeared six times to three shepherd children, Lucia Dos Santos and Francisco and Jacinta Marto. She revealed herself as "Our Lady of the Rosary" and asked for prayer and conversion in the lives of all God's people.

# Jesus and the Rosary

When we are finished praying the Rosary, we realize that we have relived the life of Jesus. Jesus comes alive again in our minds and our hearts as we say the Rosary. We are reminded again that Jesus will be with us in the joyful times of our lives and in the times that are sorrowful.

We recall, too, the promise of Jesus to us if we are faithful to him in our lives. He has promised that he will bring us to a glorious time where we, too, will be welcomed to God's presence — heaven — forever.

May we pray the life of Jesus again and again all through our lives. May the Rosary bring us very close to Mary and to her son, Jesus.